Free Fall

as told to Pat Quinn

Learning Media

Contents

I'd Love to Do That!

One day, when I was seventeen, I was waiting at the airport for my mother. I looked up, and … "Wow that is so amazing!" A parachute was floating in the sky above me. I could see someone hanging underneath it, steering it down to land. "I'd love to do that," I thought.

My friends and family said I was crazy. "You'll never do that. It's too dangerous!" But I really wanted to do it … and I did! It took six weeks of training before I was allowed to do my first jump, but it finally happened. That's me there!

I learned to jump from a plane, high in the sky. The higher I was, the more time I had. I could free-fall – swoop and fly through the air – in the time before I had to open my chute. I learned how to join up with other skydivers in the air – first in groups of three or four, then in groups of ten.

Then with more and more people, until at last, after many years of skydiving, I was ready to try for "the big one." One hundred women in free-fall formation. It would be a new world record!

I'm on the Team

That's how I've ended up in France with the top women skydivers from around the world. Over a hundred women have been invited, but only one hundred can do the final jump for the record. The selectors have to choose the best skydivers, so we start by jumping in groups of forty people. The selectors watch videos of these jumps. It will take about a week to find out who the lucky ones are.

I'm nervous. I've come all the way from the other side of the world, so I want to be part of the record jump … and yes! I'm on the team!

Now we have to practice for the big jump. But it's very important that we work out the jump on the ground first. We plan the formation on paper, using stamp men.

Then we do lots of dirt diving.

We practice moving into our positions. We hold onto the arms or legs of the people next to us and wait till everyone's linked up. When we're in the air, we'll be hanging onto grips — small tubes on the arms and legs of a skydiver's jumpsuit.

The skydivers are from all over the world, so our organizer speaks lots of languages. He talks through the plan in German, French, and English to make sure everyone knows what they have to do.

Dirt diving is where we practice getting into the right positions on the ground. Each skydiver has a different job and a different position. We plan where we'll go so that we don't get in each other's way. You can't talk when you're in free fall because the wind snatches your words away. So it's really important that we get the formation working just right on the ground before we try it in the air.

Now we practice from the planes. To do the jump with one hundred people, we have to jump from very high up to give us time to build the formation.

We practice the jump, first with sixty people, then with eighty.

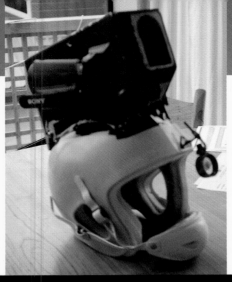

After each jump, we watch the videos to work out what we're doing right and what's going wrong.

It's hot, and the gusty winds are making it hard to land safely. Five people have already hurt themselves landing. This means they can't do the jump, and we have to choose other divers to replace them. And you get *so* tired – there's not much oxygen in the air that high up. But we have to keep practicing.

We jump with eighty-five people, then eighty-six, then ninety-five.

At last we're ready to do the formation with one hundred people.

Breathe Deeply

*T*his is it! I'm sitting in the plane, trying to relax. There are five planes, each big enough to drive a car into. Today, each plane carries twenty skydivers and the camera operators. I sit on one of the jump seats along the sides of the plane. I'm nervous. I close my eyes and breathe deeply to help relax. The planes climb higher. It's noisy, so we don't talk much. We sit quietly and think about each part of the jump.

Normal passenger planes are sealed shut so that people can breathe easily. But we're going to jump out of the planes in midair, so the planes can't be sealed ... and the higher the planes fly, the thinner the air will be. At 10 000 feet, we have to take oxygen to help us breathe. We share one mask between three of us.

I breathe the oxygen in two or three times, then pass it to the next person. I sit back and think about the jump – how the formation will look as I fly down to it, and how it will build up from the middle. I have to look for a block of people in green. The person I'll be joining up with has a black jumpsuit with pink grips.

16

There's a person in charge on each plane. In the "lead" plane, the person in charge will be looking out of the window for the white spot on the ground. That spot marks where we have to jump out. The pilot in the lead plane passes instructions on to the other planes. The pilots fly very carefully. The planes are so close together that their wing tips almost touch.

"One minute!" The countdown starts at exactly the same time in each plane. The pilots begin to slow the planes to about one hundred knots. That's as slow as they can go without the engines stopping.

I stand up and check my gear. I put my goggles, gloves, and helmet on. We start moving slowly, one at a time, down the plane to the open exit door. If we all rushed at once, the plane might tip and the engines might stop.

"Thirty seconds," the leader says.

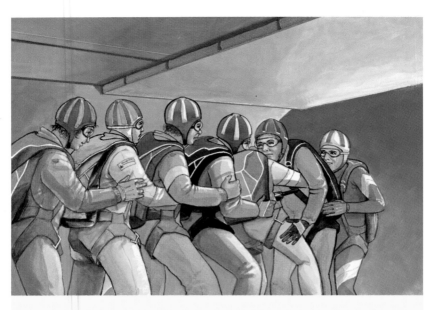

I take my position. Wow! This is it!

"OK! Are we going to get this, girls?"
someone says.

"Yeah! We're going to
get it!" we shout.

"Ten seconds."

I take a few
deep breaths.

"OK – go!"

Three Seconds

I run out of the plane as fast as I can. The heaviest divers have already jumped out. Heavy skydivers fall fastest, and their job is to build the middle of the formation. I'm light, so I'm on the outside. I get into the dive position, hands held back, legs straight, head down.

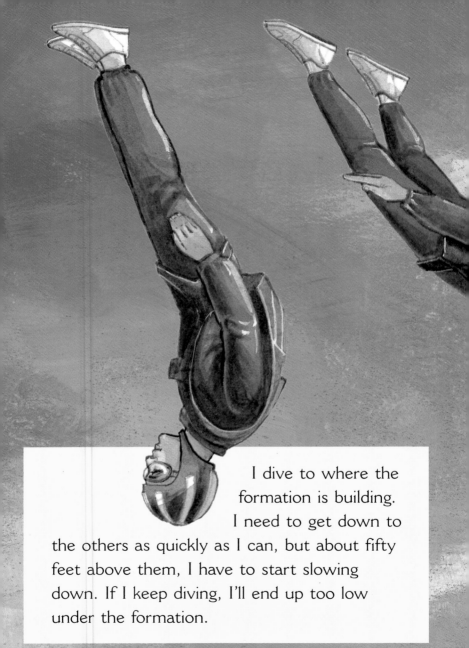

I dive to where the
formation is building.
I need to get down to
the others as quickly as I can, but about fifty
feet above them, I have to start slowing
down. If I keep diving, I'll end up too low
under the formation.

I'm still falling fast, so I slow down even more by moving my arms forward and keeping my body and legs flat. The air pushes against me. It's like a really strong wind roaring up from the earth.

I hunch over to "hug" the wind coming up at me. Now there's more of me for the wind to push against.

When I'm about ten feet above the formation, I "rest" on the wind. I do this by bending my legs back and bending my arms.

I keep out of people's way and watch the formation build, just the way we planned it on the ground. As more people join in, I get closer to my position. I sink down. I get in closer still. The person I'm going to "grip" onto flies into position. I watch as she takes hold of her grips. She's there.

Now I start flying in … slowly, slowly. If I come in too suddenly, or with a bump, the formation might collapse. I look around to check my position. Everything looks OK. I move forward carefully to take my grips. That's it. I've made it!

Now that I'm in the formation, I have to fly with it. We have to work together to keep the formation level and flat. If parts of it begin to droop or slide away, people won't be able to hold their grips.

To set a new record, we have to have exactly one hundred people in the formation. We have to hold the formation for at least three seconds.

Can we do it? From the corner of my eye, I can see the camera operators. They've been waiting further out, and now they begin flying in. This means the formation is complete!

One hundred women in free fall!

The camera operators come in really close. Some fly under us on their backs. Others film us from above.

"Yahoo! Yeah!" we yell. We're all so excited to be free-falling ... but have we got the record?

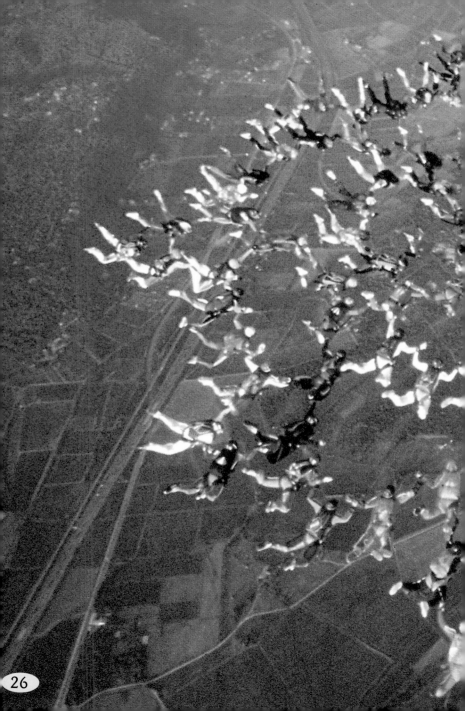

Breaking Off

*I*t's time to break off. This can be dangerous because there are so many of us in the air. We're falling very fast toward the ground. When we were dirt diving on the ground before the jump, we'd planned how and when we'd let go of the formation. We'd planned how we would fly away from each other, open our parachutes, and get safely to the ground without bumping into each other.

At 5000 feet above the ground, the skydivers in the middle begin kicking their legs. That's the sign for the outside layer to drop their grips.

I let go and turn away from the formation. I want to get away fast. But I don't want to drop too far, or I'll run into the next layer of divers as they fly away from the formation. I move my arms and legs into a tracking position.

Even when we've opened our parachutes and we're drifting down toward the ground, we're still very close together. I look around all the time. Where are the skydivers above me? How far am I from the ones below? We fly our parachutes very carefully.

As we land, people clap and cheer. We go into a room with the judges. There are big TV screens, and the judges watch the videos carefully. This is to make sure everyone's in the right place and no one has let go for those three important seconds.

Then the judges announce the result. Yes! It's a new world record. One hundred women in free-fall formation. And we held it for seven seconds! That's four more seconds than we needed for the record.

It's been very hard work. We're all really tired, but already I'm thinking about what I'd like to do next. Freestyle free-fall sounds good. It's like ballet in the air. One day, I might go to Oregon and do a jump from a balloon. I could practice my freestyle moves. If I could just find someone to take photographs ....

Clothing

Helmet – made of leather, keeps hair out of the eyes and face, and protects the skydiver from knocks

Goggles – protect eyes and stop them stinging

Jumpsuit – light, so that you can move through the air fast

Flying Positions

As a skydiver falls through the air, it rushes past her body. The most basic flying position is the box position. The skydiver balances with her head up, hands in front, and legs bent. The skydiver is "resting" on the wind.

To fall faster, the skydiver arches up, lifting her arms back and legs higher so that less body surface is presented to the air.

A steeper glide is a dive.

To slow down, the skydiver needs to "catch" the air flowing past her body. She straightens out her legs, drops her arms, and hunches her body.